Clarinet Book 3

PREMIER PERFORMANCE

AN INNOVATIVE AND COMPREHENSIVE BAND METHOD

by Ed Sueta

Dear Band Student:

Welcome to Book Three of ***Premier Performance!*** *Congratulations on your successful completion of Book One and Book Two.*

You are to be commended on your continued commitment to master your instrument. The further you advance your study, the more exciting opportunities await you. Be proud of your accomplishments and enjoy Book Three!

Best wishes for musical success!

Ed Sueta

Instruments provided courtesy
of **The Selmer Company, Inc.**

PREMIER TECHNIQUE

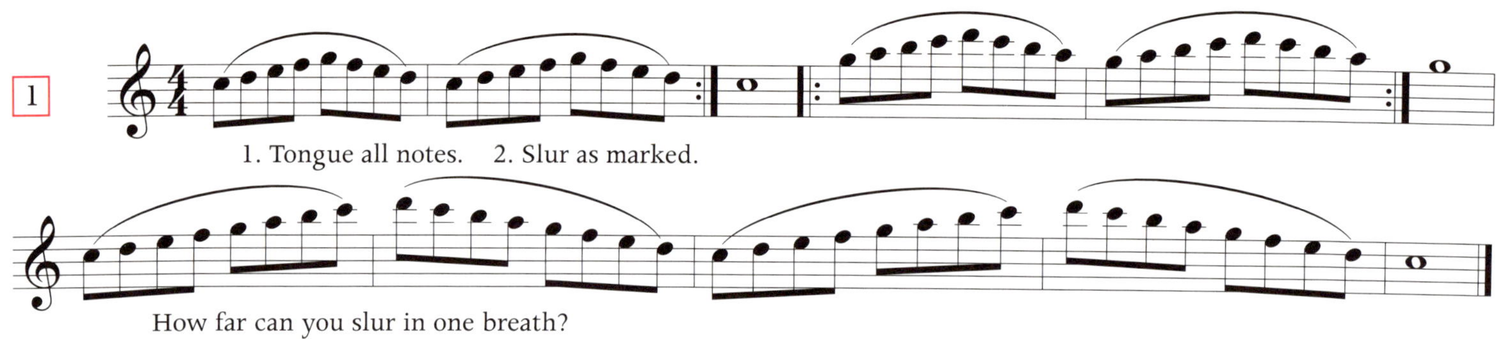

1

1. Tongue all notes. 2. Slur as marked.
How far can you slur in one breath?

SCOTTISH DANCE

Traditional

2

Allegretto
mf
Gradual accelerando to the end

CUMBERLAND MOUNTAIN DEER CHASE

American Pioneer Song

3

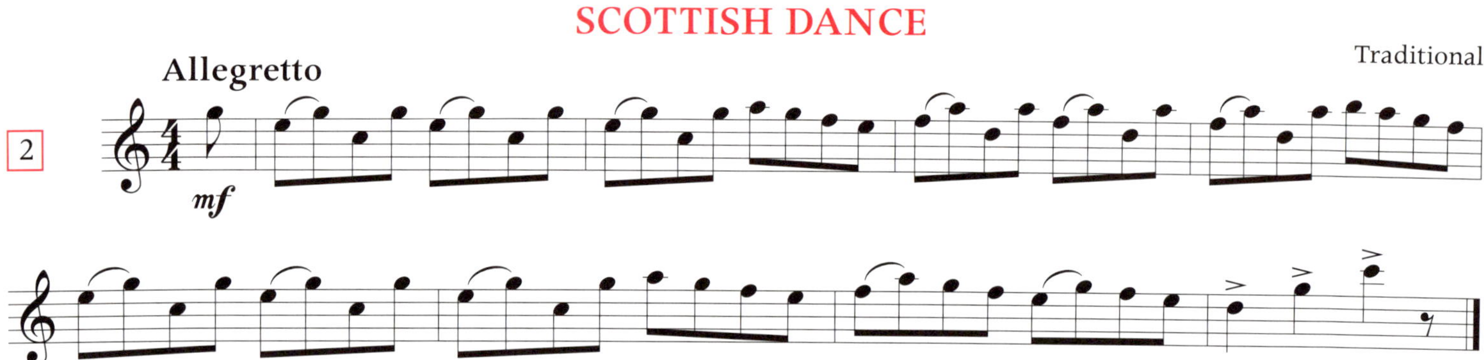

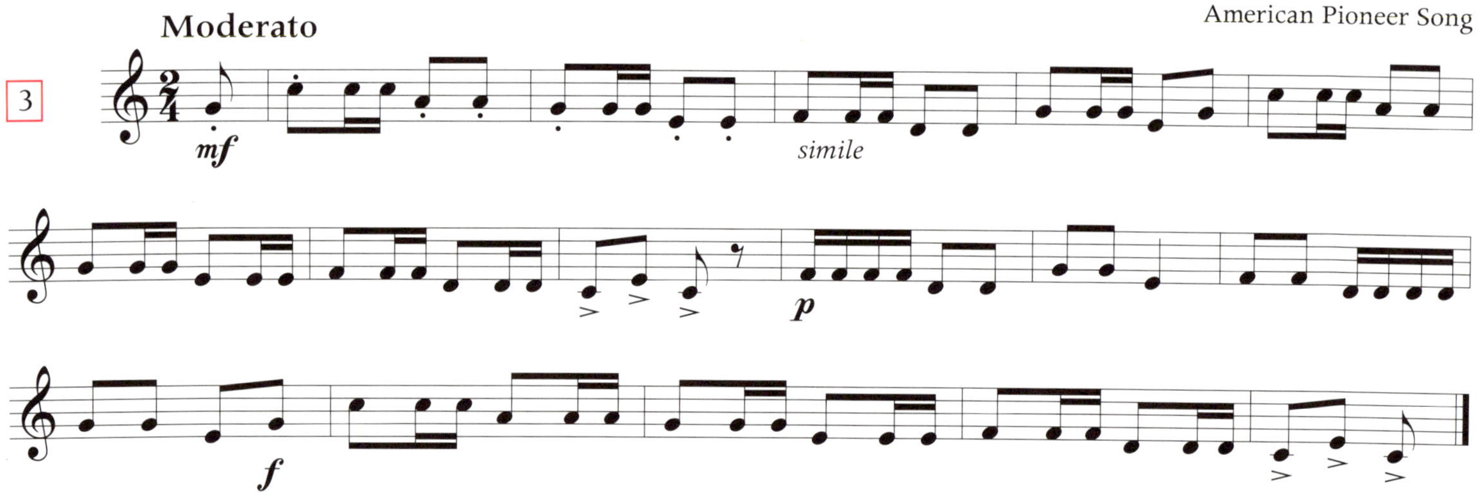
Moderato
mf
simile
p
f

BOHEMIAN POLKA

Traditional

4

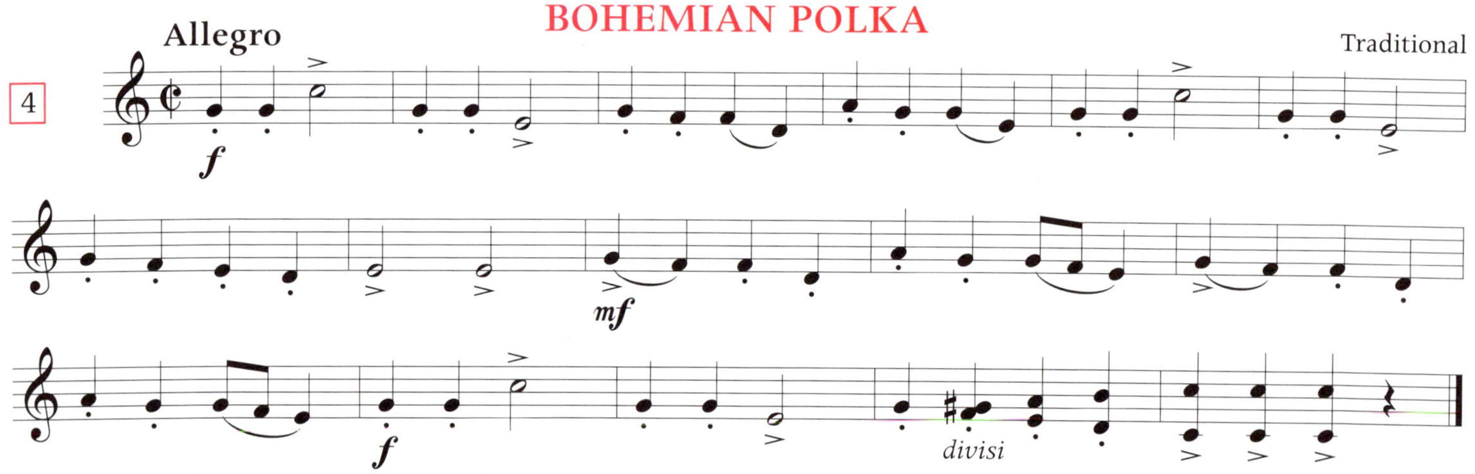
Allegro
f
mf
f
divisi

Your teacher will assign the Premier Rhythm Lines on pages 32-35 as you play through this book.

NATIONAL EMBLEM

PREMIER TECHNIQUE

8

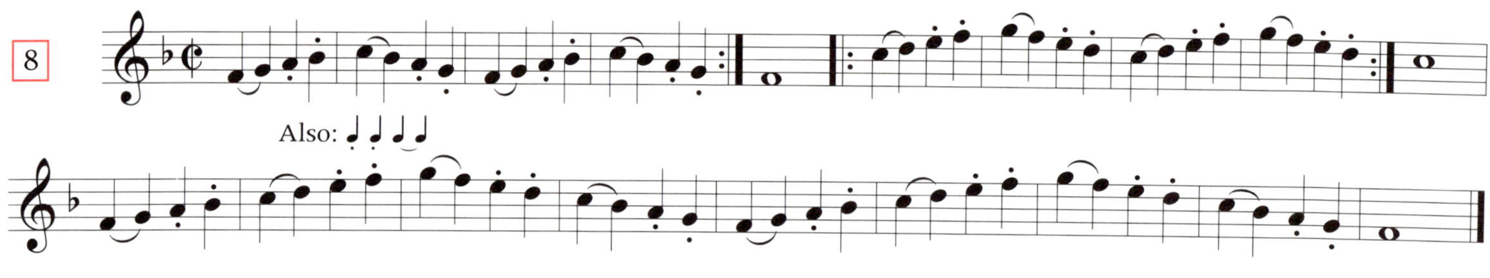

WINTER FROM THE FOUR SEASONS

Antonio Vivaldi
(1678-1741)

Largo

9

mp *legato*

CALYPSO

Allegretto

Ed Sueta

10

mf

3rd ending on the *D.S.*

1.

2., 3. *Fine*

D.S. al Fine

p

mf

MICHAEL FINNEGAN

Con spirito

Traditional English

11

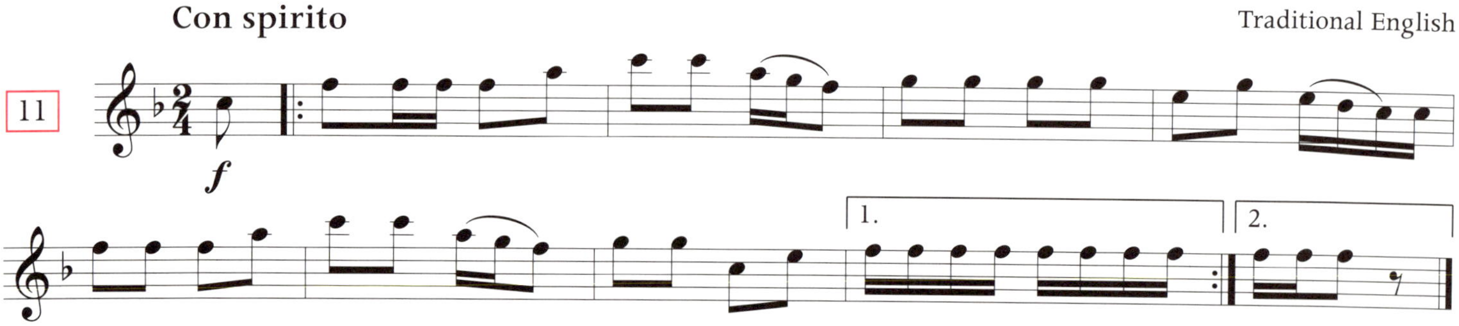

f

1.

2.

THIS LITTLE LIGHT OF MINE

Spiritual

Play Premier Technique Line 2 on page 36.

PREMIER TECHNIQUE
16
Also:
Start with your right hand fingers down on G.
HORN CONCERTO No. 4 EXCERPT
Wolfgang Amadeus Mozart
(1756-1791)
Allegro
17
p
No repeat on the D.C.
Fine
mf
D.C. al Fine
HAIL, HAIL, THE GANG'S ALL HERE
Camp Song
Allegretto
18
f
THEME FROM CHORAL FANTASIA
Ludwig van Beethoven
(1770-1827)
Moderato
19
mf legato
mp
mp
mf

ALONG THE ROAD TO GUNDAGAI

MEXICAN FOLK DANCE

THE SLEIGH RIDE

Play Premier Technique Line 3 on page 36.

CZECH FOLK DANCE
Traditional
Allegro
23
mf
f
f
FINLANDIA
Jean Sibelius
(1865-1957)
Andante
24
mf with expression
1.
2.
MARCH FROM THE OPERA CARMEN
Georges Bizet
(1838-1875)
Allegro Giocoso
25
f
simile

GOPAK
Belorussian Dance
Allegretto
26
Fine
mf
Play the repeat on the D.C.
f
1.
2.
D.C. al Fine
ALLELUIA - ROUND
Wolfgang Amadeus Mozart
(1756-1791)
Allegretto
27
1
mf
2
3
FLOWING RIVER
Chilean Folk Song
Moderato
28
p
legato
p
gradual crescendo
f
p
EASY WINNERS
Scott Joplin
(1868-1917)
Not fast
29
mf

PREMIER TECHNIQUE

PIANO CONCERTO THEME
Edvard Grieg
(1843-1907)
Moderato
34
p
dolce
p
POLKA
Peter Ilyich Tchaikovsky
(1840-1893)
Moderato
35
mp
mp
DANCE FROM CARMEN
Georges Bizet
(1838-1875)
Allegretto
36
pp
f
p
f
f
MARCH FROM THE NUTCRACKER SUITE
Peter Ilyich Tchaikovsky
(1840-1893)
Tempo di marcia viva
37
p
mf
p
mf
p
crescendo
f

Play Premier Technique Line 4 on page 36.

WELSH FOLK SONG

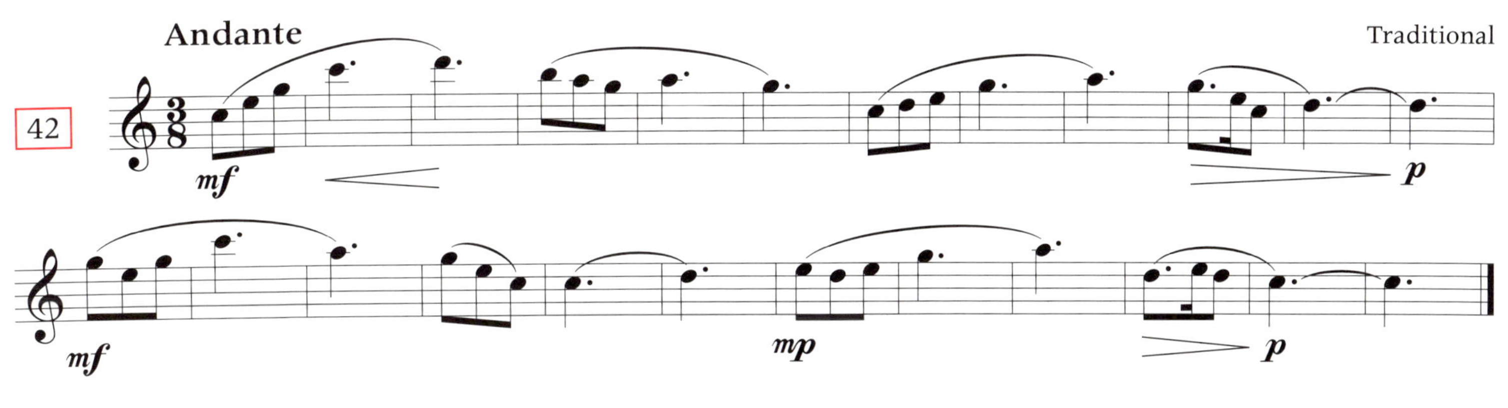

O CANADA

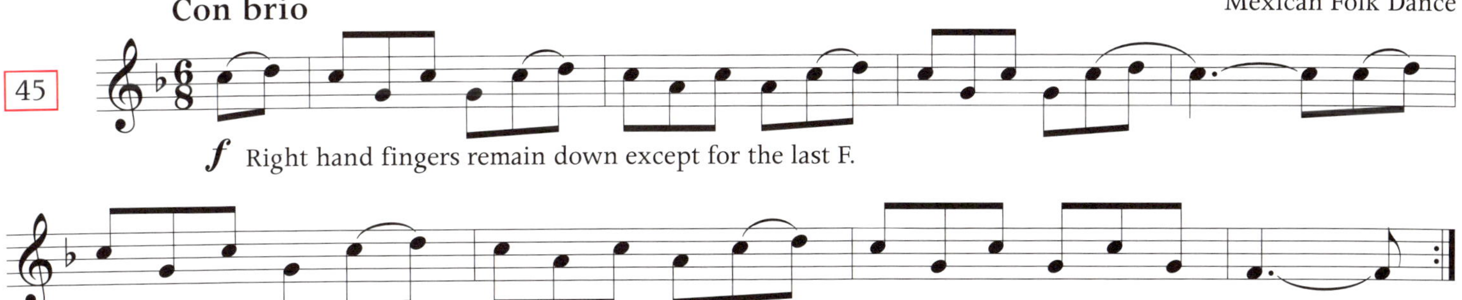

PREMIER TECHNIQUE

46

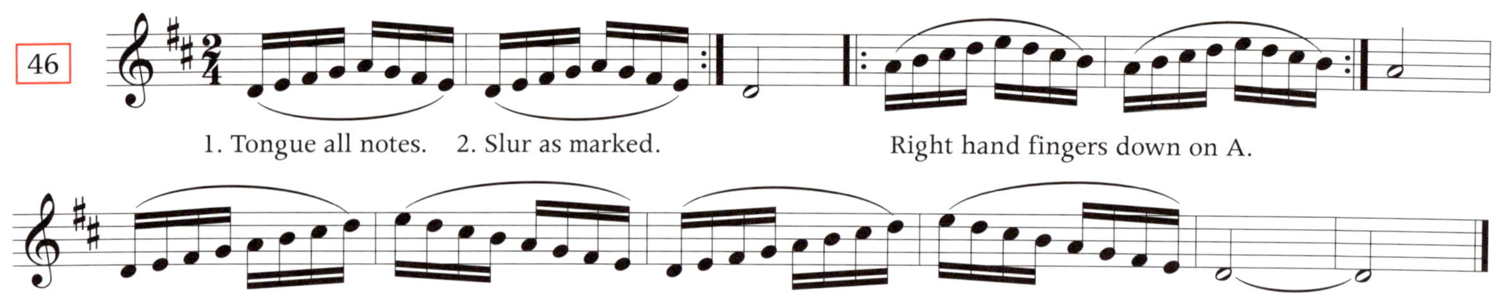

TA-RA-RA-BOOM-TE-AY

College Song

47

JAMAICA FAREWELL

Caribbean Calypso

48

TZENA, TZENA
Israeli Folk Song
Allegro
49
mf
f
mp
f
1.
2.
THE LINDEN TREE
German Folk Song
C♯
Andante
50
mp legato
C♯
mf
HIGH POINT MARCH
Ed Sueta
Moderato
51
f
mf
1.
2.
ST. PATRICK´S DAY
Irish Jig
Allegro
52
mf-f

LA CUCARACHA

GAVOTTE

Arcangelo Corelli
(1653-1713)

JAZZ BLUES PROGRESSION

Not too fast

♫ = ♩♪ (triplet) Your teacher will explain.

Play Premier Technique Line 5 on page 36.

ADVANCE AUSTRALIA FAIR

Peter Dodds McCormick
(1834-1916)

SAILOR´S HORNPIPE

English Shanty

SARIE MARAIS MARCH

South African March

SEE THE CONQUERING HERO COME

FROM JUDAS MACCABAEUS

George Frederic Handel
(1685-1759)

MANANITAS TAPATIAS

Mexican Folk Song

BLUES SCALE ROCK

Ed Sueta

PREMIER TECHNIQUE
62
mf-p
Also:
mf-p
mf-p
mf-p
MARCH FROM AIDA
Allegro Maestoso
Giuseppe Verdi
(1813-1901)
63
mf
Play the repeat on the D.S.
1.
2., 3.
Fine
p
D.S. al Fine
SAMBALE
Moderato
Brazilian Folk Dance
64
mf
Fine
divisi
f
D.C. al Fine
NO HIDING PLACE
Lively
Spiritual
65
mf
L

ARGENTINIAN MARCH

Army Field March

C´EST L´AVIRON

PULL ON THE OARS

French Canadian Folk Song

LINSTEAD MARKET

West Indian Folk Song

JAZZ BLUES

EVERY NIGHT WHEN THE SUN GOES IN

ENGLISH SHANTY

Play Premier Technique Line 6 on page 37.

DOWN IN DEMERARA

STODOLA POMPA

ANDALUSIA

Play Premier Technique Lines 7 and 8 on page 37.

MARCH

George Frederic Handel
(1685-1759)

MEXICAN CAROL

Traditional

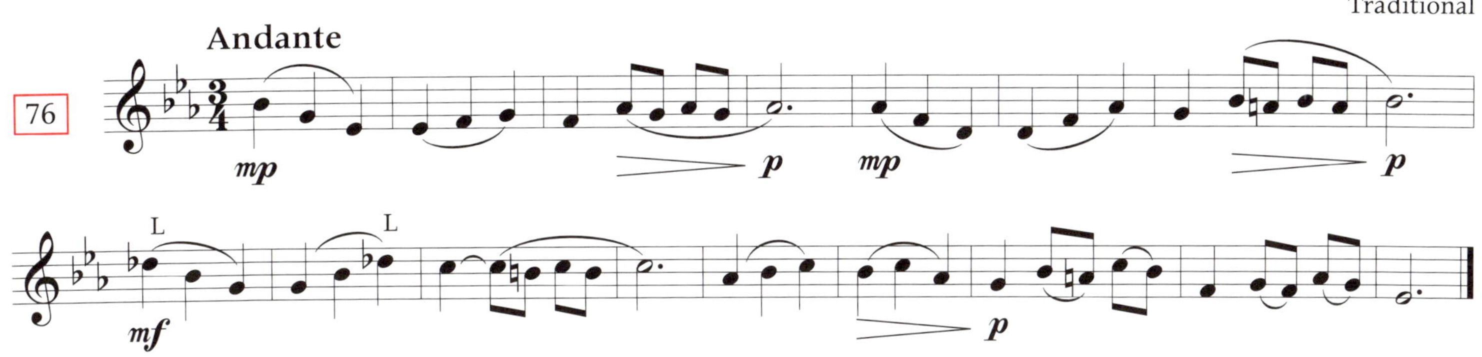

HERE WE COME A´WASSAILING

Old English Tune

Play Premier Technique Line 9 on page 37.

LA JESUCITA

Mexican Folk Dance

THE KERRY DANCE

Traditional Irish

KATIOUCHKA

Russian Cossack Dance

EXCERPT FROM THE PEASANT CANTATA

Johann Sebastian Bach
(1685-1750)

RULE BRITANNIA

Thomas Arne
(1710-1778)

TINGA LAYO

West Indian Folk Tune

AH! SI MON MOINE VOULAIT DANSER!

COME DANCE WITH ME!

IRISH JIG

EXCERPT FROM "EINE KLEINE NACHTMUSIK"

Play Premier Technique Line 10 on page 37.

TRUMPET MINUET

Jeremiah Clarke
(1674-1707)

HYMN OF THE SLAVS

Old Bohemian Song

LA RASPA

Mexican Folk Dance

LAID BACK BLUES

Medium Jazz Tempo

Ed Sueta

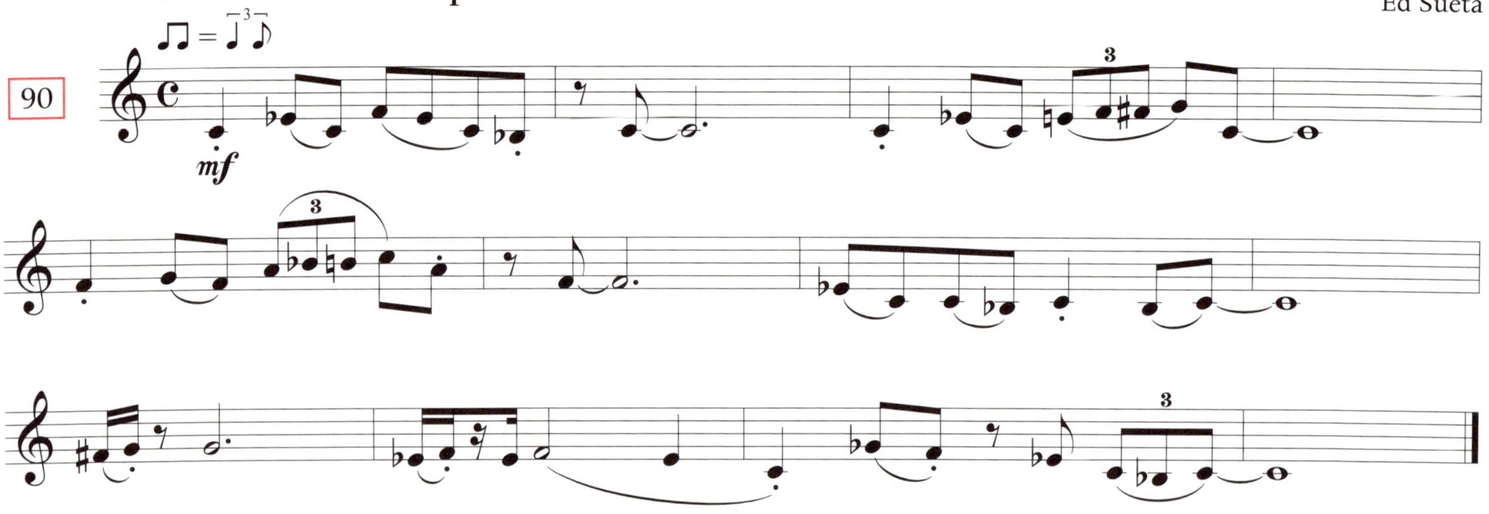
90
mf
3

TARANTELLA

Con spirito

Traditional Italian Dance

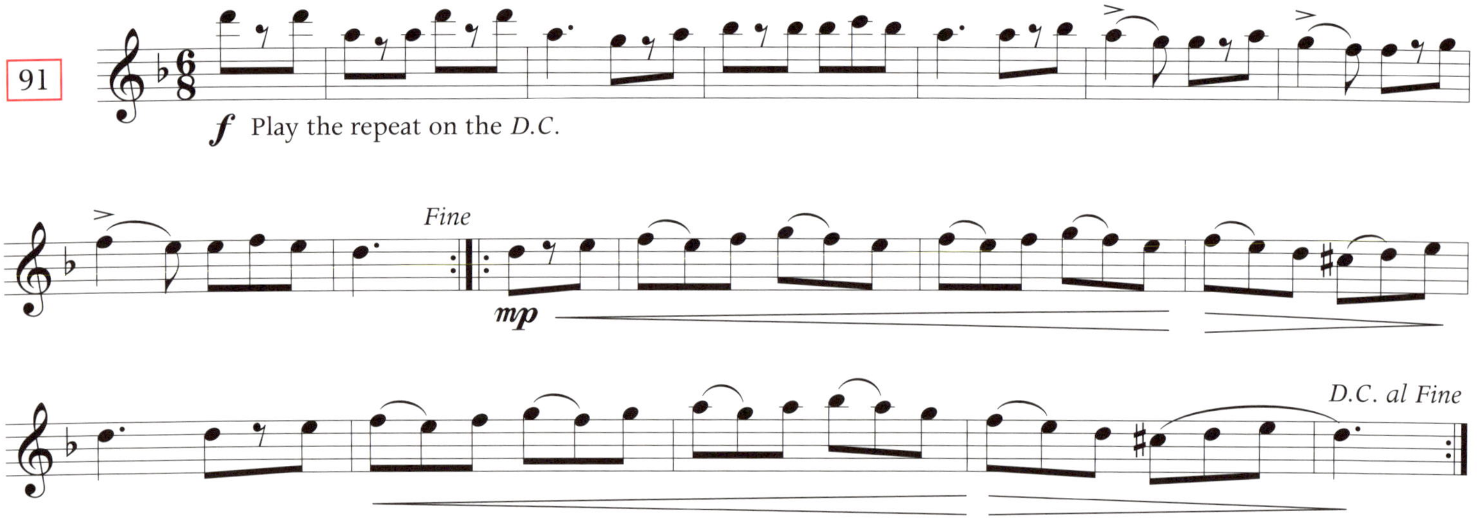
91
f Play the repeat on the D.C.
Fine
mp
D.C. al Fine

NORWEGIAN DANCE No. 2

Edvard Grieg
(1843-1907)

Allegretto

92
mf
mp
mf
rit.

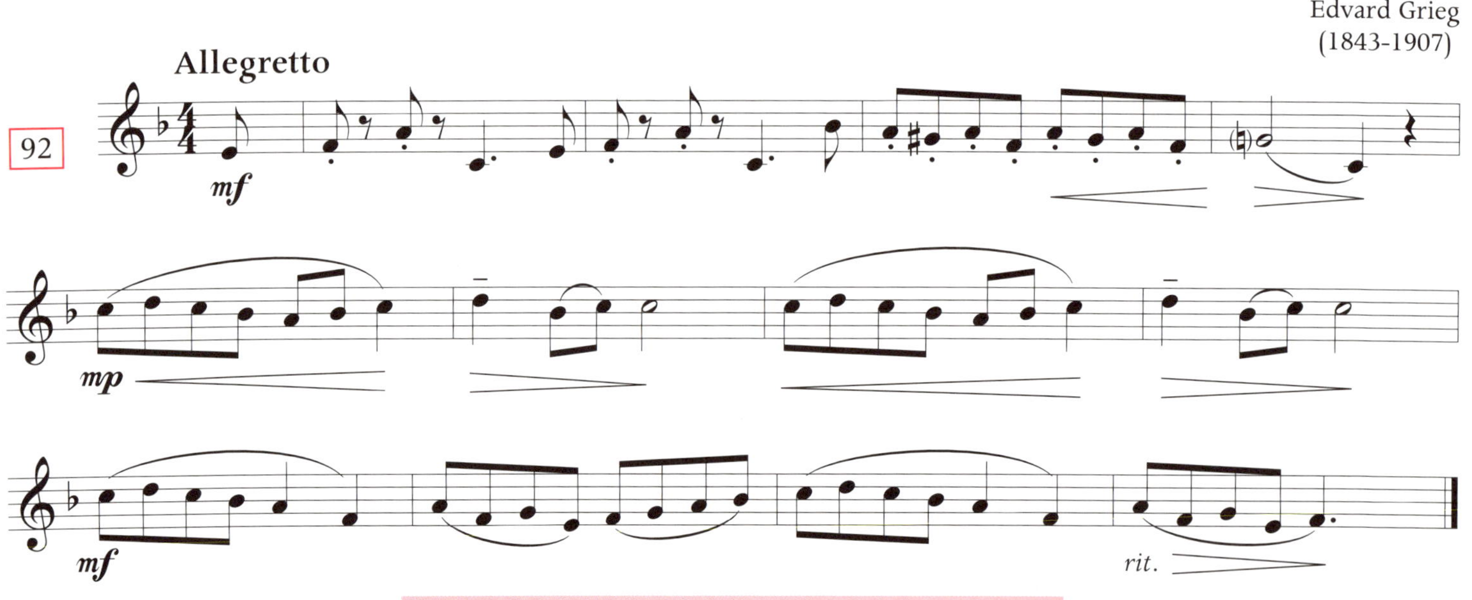

Play Premier Technique Line 11 on page 37.

THREE PATRIOTIC SONGS

YOU´RE A GRAND OLD FLAG

George M. Cohan
(1878-1942)

THE STARS AND STRIPES FOREVER

John Philip Sousa
(1854-1932)

STAR SPANGLED BANNER

Words by
Francis Scott Key
(1750-1836)

Composer Unknown

PREMIER MAJOR AND MINOR SCALES - ARPEGGIOS

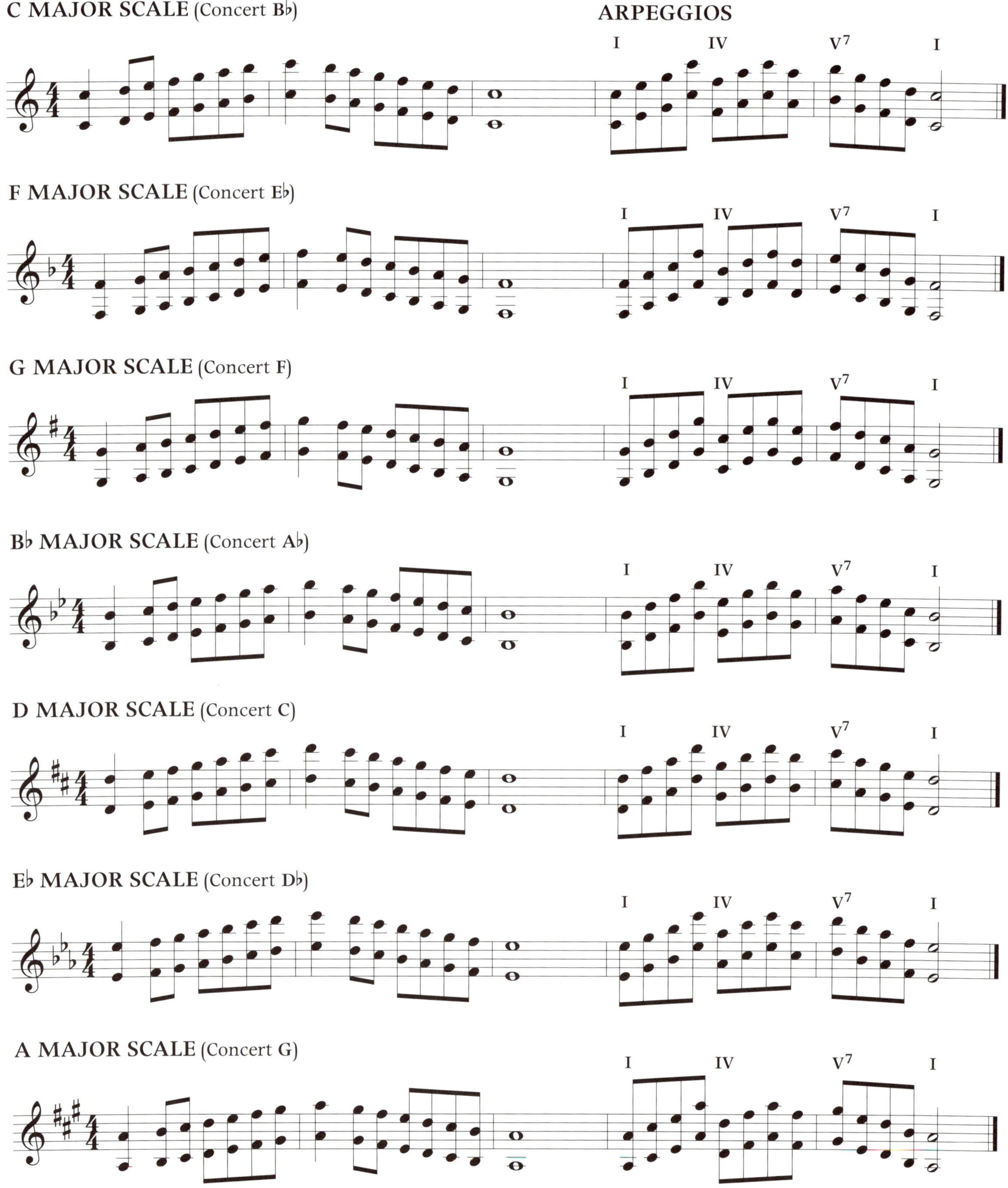

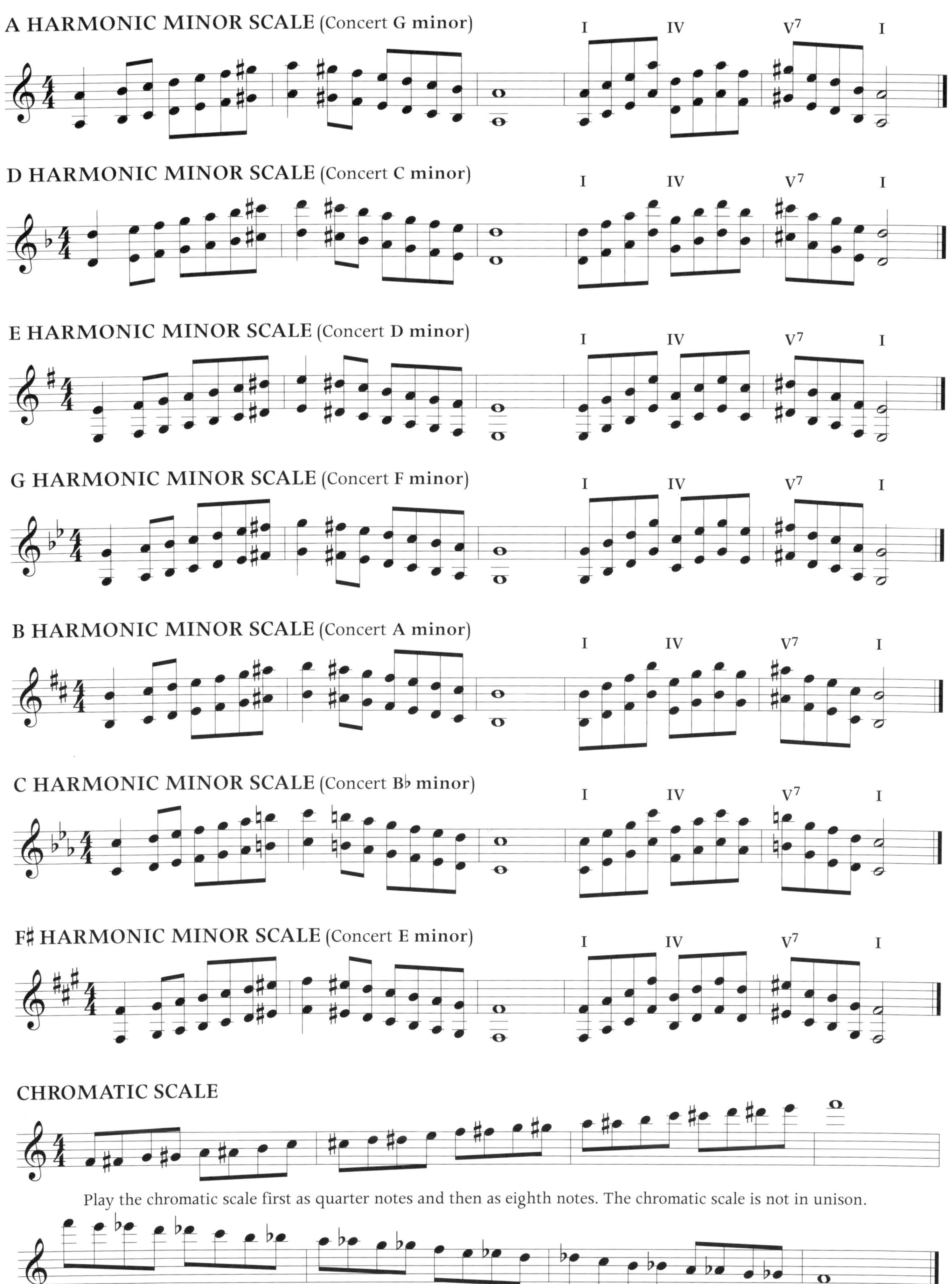
A HARMONIC MINOR SCALE (Concert G minor)
I IV V7 I
D HARMONIC MINOR SCALE (Concert C minor)
I IV V7 I
E HARMONIC MINOR SCALE (Concert D minor)
I IV V7 I
G HARMONIC MINOR SCALE (Concert F minor)
I IV V7 I
B HARMONIC MINOR SCALE (Concert A minor)
I IV V7 I
C HARMONIC MINOR SCALE (Concert B♭ minor)
I IV V7 I
F♯ HARMONIC MINOR SCALE (Concert E minor)
I IV V7 I
CHROMATIC SCALE
Play the chromatic scale first as quarter notes and then as eighth notes. The chromatic scale is not in unison.

PREMIER RHYTHMS

1. Tap the beat with your left hand and the notes with your right hand.
2. Reverse step one.
3. After a line becomes easy, increase your speed.
   (Left handed students can reverse steps one and two.)

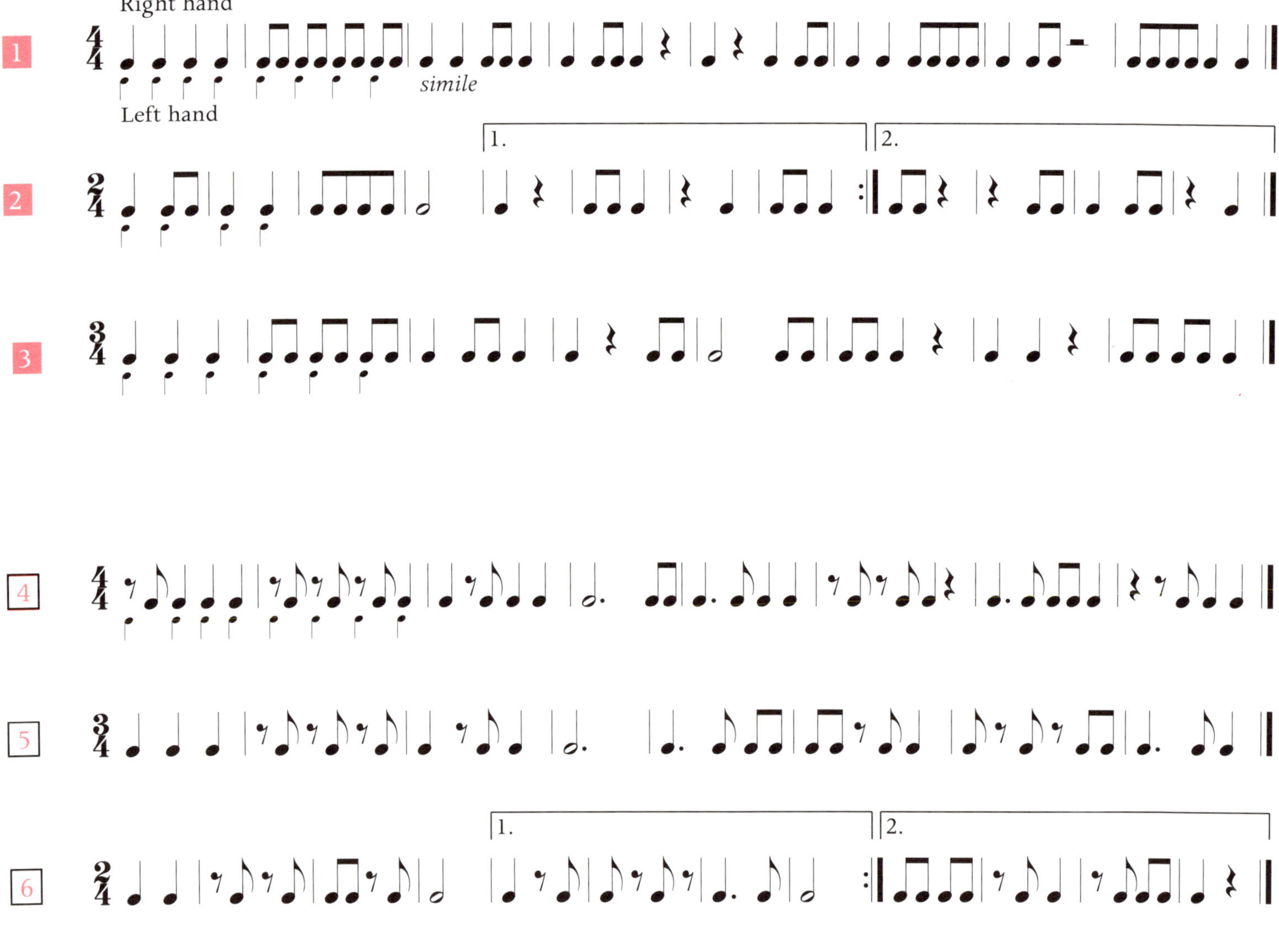

7

1. 2.

8

9

1. 2.

10

11

12

13

14

15

(6)

(2)

16

17

18

19

20

21

22

23

24

25

26

27

28

29

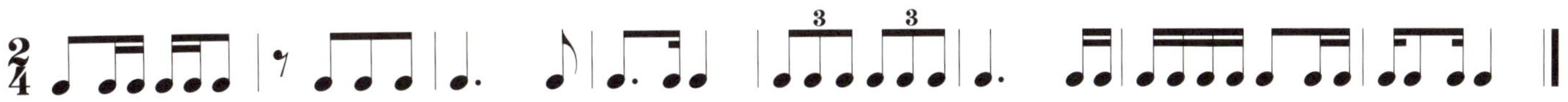

30

31

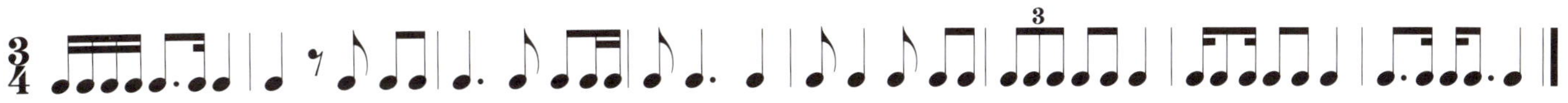

32

33

PREMIER TECHNIQUE

1. Practice the exercises **SLOWLY** at first.
2. Keep your fingers **CLOSE** to the keys and bring them down with precision in order to develop strength and evenness.
3. Play only as fast as you can play **ACCURATELY.**
4. Practice the exercises with a **METRONOME** to increase your speed gradually.
5. Practice the exercises with **DIFFERENT DYNAMICS:** ***mf***, ***f*** and ***p***.

6
L
1. Tongue all notes. 2. Slur as marked.
7
F♯ Alternate
1. Play repeated measures 3 times. 2. Tongue all notes. 3. Slur as marked.
8
F♯ Alternate
G♭ Alternate
1. Tongue all notes. 2. Slur as marked. 3. How far can you slur in one breath?
9
L
10
Right hand fingers down for all G's and A's
11
D♯
E♭
E
F
F♯ Alternate
For a smooth legato, slide your left index finger off the key.
Blow a fast, intense air stream. It may be helpful to raise your tongue in a "E" position and direct the air toward the roof of your mouth.

FINGERING CHART

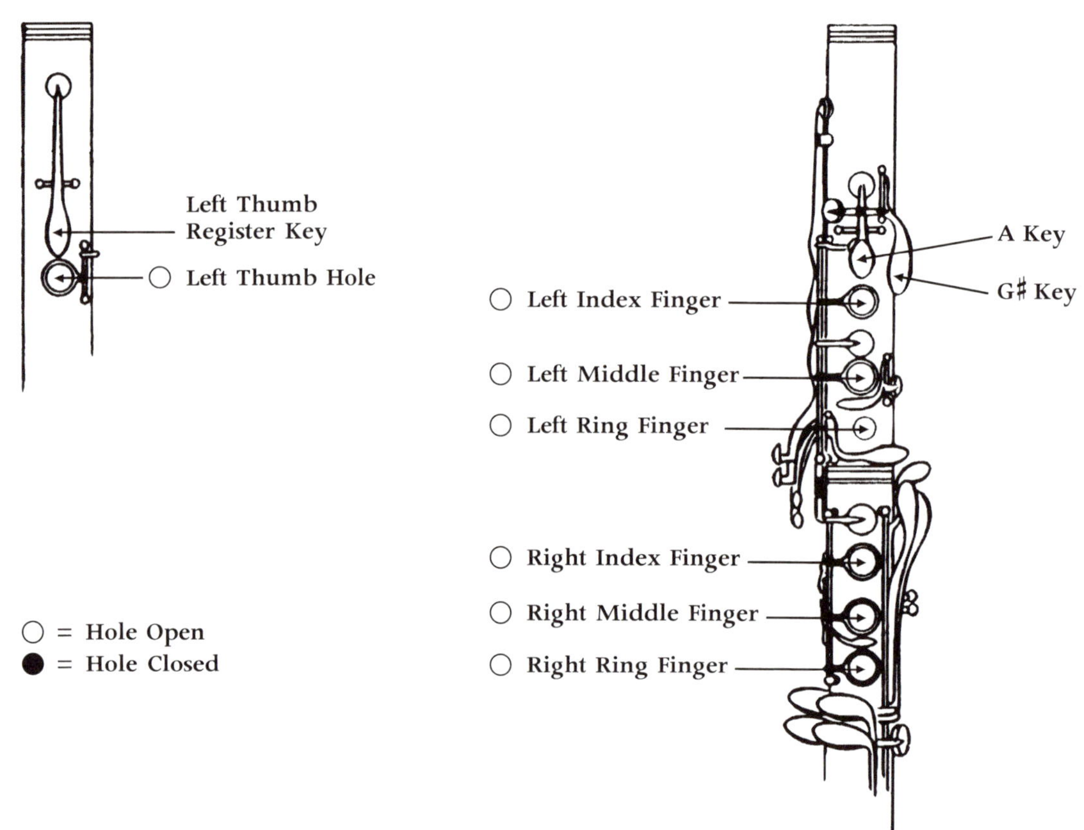

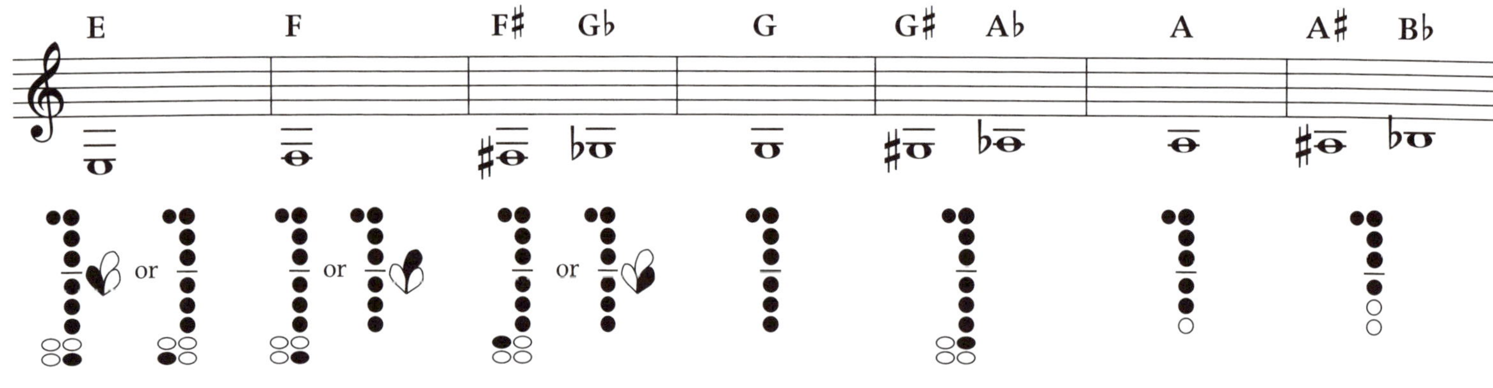

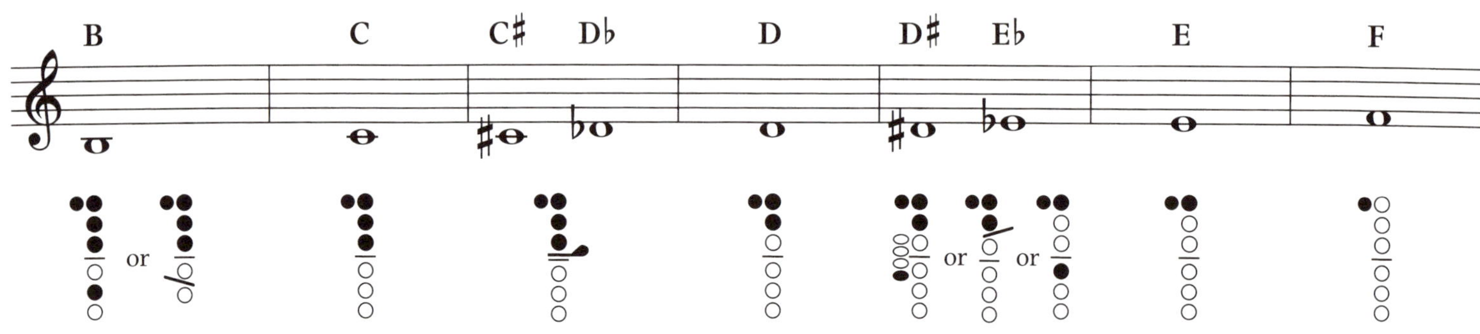

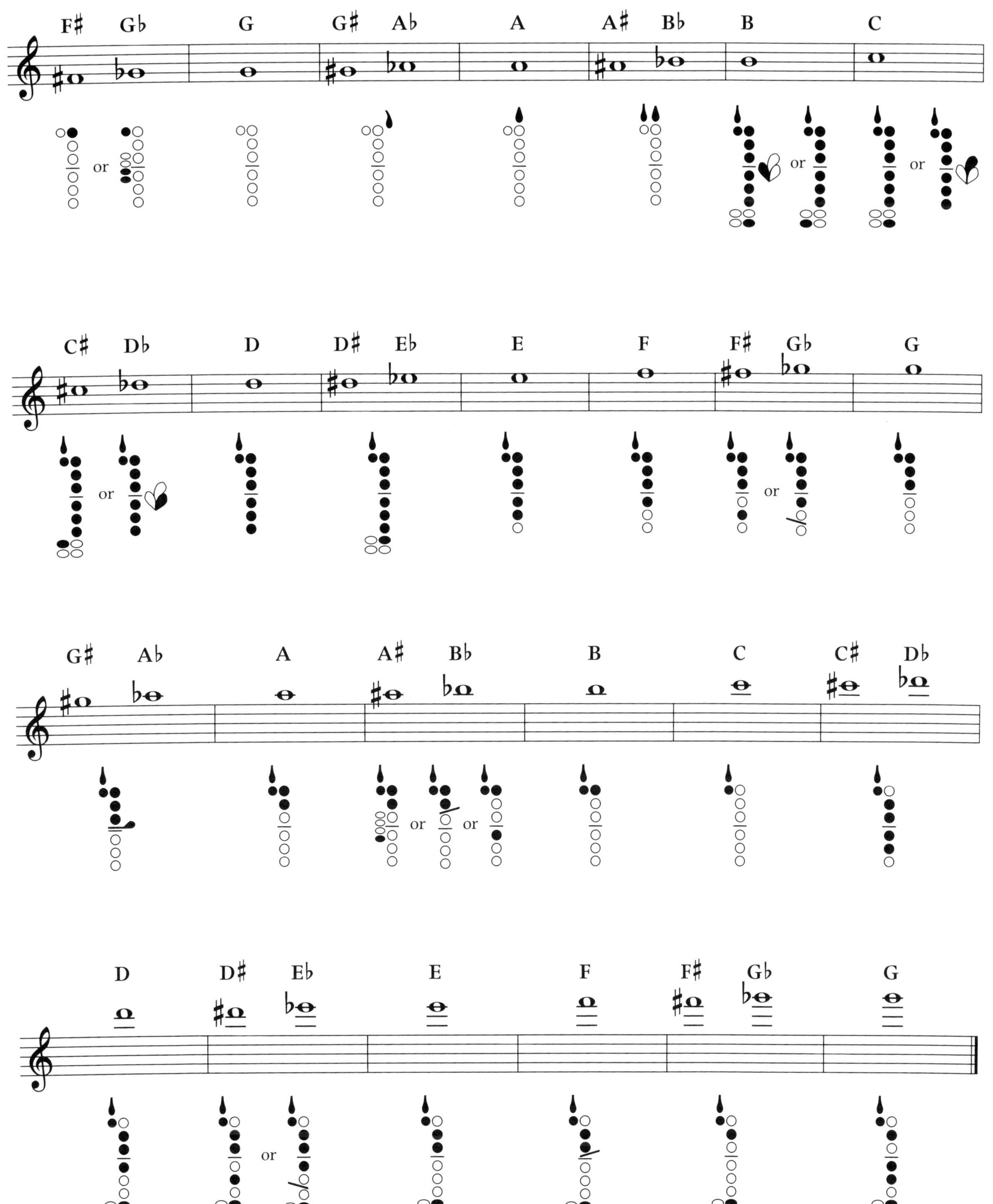
F♯ G♭
G
G♯ A♭
A
A♯ B♭
B
C
or
or
or
C♯ D♭
D
D♯ E♭
E
F
F♯ G♭
G
or
or
G♯ A♭
A
A♯ B♭
B
C
C♯ D♭
or
or
D
D♯ E♭
E
F
F♯ G♭
G
or

PREMIER PROGRESS PRACTICE CHART

DATE	ASSIGNMENT/FOCUS POINTS	M	T	W	T	F	S	S	TOTAL	PARENT SIGNATURE

QUARTERLY GRADE ________

DATE	ASSIGNMENT/FOCUS POINTS	M	T	W	T	F	S	S	TOTAL	PARENT SIGNATURE

QUARTERLY GRADE ________

DATE	ASSIGNMENT/FOCUS POINTS	M	T	W	T	F	S	S	TOTAL	PARENT SIGNATURE

QUARTERLY GRADE ________

DATE	ASSIGNMENT/FOCUS POINTS	M	T	W	T	F	S	S	TOTAL	PARENT SIGNATURE

QUARTERLY GRADE ________

FINAL GRADE ________